WHY
BARACK OBAMA
WON MY VOTE

BookSurge Publishing
www.booksurge.com
1-866-308-6235
orders@booksurge.com

TEXAS JAMES
(LEROY TAPIA)

WHY
BARACK OBAMA
WON MY VOTE

2008

WHY
BARACK OBAMA
WON MY VOTE

I dedicate this book to my two children, Lizzy and Joshua; and to the new love of my life, Norma Lizzette (a very beautiful woman); without their support this book would have not been possible; To GOD and to Barack Obama, God Bless You and God Bless America.

-Leroy (Texas James)

Preface

Barack Obama promises more handouts; can America afford them all? Yes, America can, but before that can be accomplished many things have to change. Obama has promised to bring change to America; synonyms for the word "CHANGE" is:

1. Alter
2. Modify
3. Vary
4. Transform
5. Revolutionize
6. Adjust
7. Amend
8. Alter

One key word that cannot be ignored to successfully fulfill these is "BALANCE". Balance is crucial if one is to believe that this can happen without jeopardizing high spending. The President must bring CHANGE and BALANCE to the Whitehouse, and must do so immediately. Politicians must change their huge spending tactics. Its no secret they have lobbied for there own agendas and interests for far too long now.

America has taken a backseat to the special interest groups and has been raped and violated from within…and as blunt and cold as that may sound, it doesn't accurately depict the entire wasteful spending currently taking place. Barack Obama promises to bring CHANGE to the Whitehouse, and as Americans we must hold him accountable to that promise. "Change cannot come out of Washington, it must come to Washington."

"We need leadership that sees government not as a tool to enrich well-connected friends and high-priced lobbyists, but as the defender of fairness and opportunity for every American", quote from a speech made by Barack Obama.

As a member of the Democratic minority, Barack Obama helped create legislation to control conventional weapons and promote greater public accountability in the use of our federal funds. He helped create legislation regarding lobbying and electoral fraud; climate change, nuclear terrorism, and care for our returned U.S. military soldiers.

After announcing his presidential campaign in February of 2007, Obama emphasized energy independence, withdrawing American troops from Iraq, decreasing the influence of lobbyists, and promoting universal health care as top national priorities for America.

Obama opposed early on the Bush administration's policies on Iraq. On October of, 2002, when President Bush and Congress agreed on the joint resolution authorizing the Iraq War, Senator Obama addressed the first high-profile Chicago anti-Iraq War rally in the Federal Plaza. On March 16, 2003, the day President Bush issued his 48-hour ultimatum to Saddam Hussein to leave Iraq before the U.S. invasion, Obama addressed an anti-Iraq War rally and told the crowd "It's not too late to stop the war".

In his acceptance speech in Denver he quoted, "As President, I will tap our natural gas reserves, invest in clean coal technology, and find ways to safely harness nuclear power. I'll help our auto companies re-tool, so that the fuel-efficient cars of the future are built right here in America. I'll make it easier for the American people to afford these new cars. And I'll invest $150 billion over the next decade in affordable, renewable sources of energy -- wind power and solar power and the next generation of biofuels; an investment that will lead to new industries and five million new jobs that pay well and can't ever be outsourced." -Barack Obama.

In economic affairs, he defended the social welfare policies of Franklin D. Roosevelt and opposed Republican proposals to establish private accounts for Social Security. Obama also proposes to reward teachers for performance from the traditional merit pay systems. Obama supports universal healthcare in the United States and stated that if elected he would enact budget cuts in the range of tens of billions of dollars.

America, it is our duty to bring change to our country, and as Americans we do have a choice. I cannot emphasize enough, learn the topics and issues don't let second hand gossip dictate who the better candidate is; learn for yourself and make a wise and informed decision.

In this book I share with you some very important topics; information gathered after months of research; you will read speeches, quotes, and an insight look of why Barack Obama Won My Vote.

-TEXAS JAMES (Leroy Tapia)

Chapter One

THE POWER OF A SPEECH

Why Barack Obama won my vote; for the first time in my life and out of desperation to the last eight years of President Bush, I decided to explore in depth all candidates for the 2008 Presidential election. Knowledge is the key to any wise decision, regardless of the unforeseen outcome. Knowledge comes as a direct action of your pursuit for a better understanding of what you know nothing about; RE: 2008 Presidential nominees, −what they stand for, track record, morals and beliefs.

The sad truth is that many Americans decide in as little as thirty seconds who they will vote for and as a direct consequence of influence by others, rather than from knowledge they obtained themselves. The knowledge I gained in my research of the candidates influenced my own personal vote for Obama as President of the United States of America.

In this book I share with you some very important topics; information gathered after months of research; you will read speeches, quotes, and an insight look of why Barack Obama Won My Vote.

The following is the 2008 Democratic nomination acceptance speech made by Barack Obama in Denver.

"To Chairman Dean and my great friend Dick Durbin; and to all my fellow citizens of this great nation; with profound gratitude and great humility, I accept your nomination for the presidency of the United States.

Let me express my thanks to the historic slate of candidates who accompanied me on this journey, and especially the one who traveled the farthest -- a champion for working Americans and an inspiration to my daughters and to yours -- Hillary Rodham Clinton. To President Clinton, who last night made the case for change as only he can make it; to Ted Kennedy, who embodies the spirit of service; and to the next Vice President of the United States, Joe Biden, I thank you. I am grateful to finish this journey with one of the finest statesmen of our time, a man at ease with everyone from world leaders to the conductors on the Amtrak train he still takes home every night.

To the love of my life, our next First Lady, Michelle Obama, and to Sasha and Malia -- I love you so much, and I'm so proud of all of you.

Four years ago, I stood before you and told you my story -- of the brief union between a young man from Kenya and a young woman from Kansas who weren't well-off or well-known, but shared a belief that in America, their son could achieve whatever he put his mind to.

It is that promise that has always set this country apart -- that through hard work and sacrifice, each of us can pursue our individual dreams but still come together as one American family, to ensure that the next generation can pursue their dreams as well.

That's why I stand here tonight. Because for two hundred and thirty two years, at each moment when that promise was in jeopardy, ordinary men and women - students and soldiers, farmers and teachers, nurses and janitors -- found the courage to keep it alive.

We meet at one of those defining moments - a moment when our nation is at war, our economy is in turmoil, and the American promise has been threatened once more.

Tonight, more Americans are out of work and more are working harder for less. More of you have lost your homes and even more are watching your home values plummet. More of you have cars you can't afford to drive, credit card bills you can't afford to pay, and tuition that's beyond your reach.

These challenges are not all of government's making. But the failure to respond is a direct result of a broken politics in Washington and the failed policies of George W. Bush. America, we are better than these last eight years. We are a better country than this. This country is more decent than one where a woman in Ohio, on the brink of retirement, finds herself one illness away from disaster after a lifetime of hard work.

This country is more generous than one where a man in Indiana has to pack up the equipment he's worked on for twenty years and watch it shipped off to China, and then chokes up as he explains how he felt like a failure when he went home to tell his family the news.

We are more compassionate than a government that lets veterans sleep on our streets and families slide into poverty; that sits on its hands while a major American city drowns before our eyes.

Tonight, I say to the American people, to Democrats and Republicans and Independents across this great land - enough! This moment - this election - is our chance to keep, in the 21st century, the American promise alive. Because next week, in Minnesota, the same party that brought you two terms of George Bush and Dick Cheney will ask this country for a third. And we are here because we love this country too much to let the next four years look like the last eight. On November 4th, we must stand up and say: "Eight is enough."

Now let there be no doubt. The Republican nominee, John McCain, has worn the uniform of our country with bravery and distinction, and for that we owe him our gratitude and respect. And next week, we'll also hear about those occasions when he's broken with his party as evidence that he can deliver the change that we need.

But the record's clear: John McCain has voted with George Bush ninety percent of the time. Senator McCain likes to talk about judgment, but really, what does it say about your judgment when you think George Bush has been right more than ninety percent of the time? I don't know about you, but I'm not ready to take a ten percent chance on change.

The truth is, on issue after issue that would make a difference in your lives - on health care and education and the economy - Senator McCain has been anything but independent. He said that our economy has made "great progress" under this President. He said that the fundamentals of the economy are strong. And when one of his chief advisors - the man who wrote his economic plan - was talking about the anxiety Americans are feeling, he said that we were just suffering from a "mental recession," and that we've become, and I quote, "a nation of whiners."

A nation of whiners? Tell that to the proud auto workers at a Michigan plant who, after they found out it was closing, kept showing up every day and working as hard as ever, because they knew there were people who counted on the brakes that they made. Tell that to the military families who shoulder their burdens silently as they watch their loved ones leave for their third or fourth or fifth tour of duty. These are not whiners. They work hard and give back and keep going without complaint. These are the Americans that I know.

Now, I don't believe that Senator McCain doesn't care what's going on in the lives of Americans. I just think he doesn't know. Why else would he define middle-class as someone making under five million dollars a year? How else could he propose hundreds of billions in tax breaks for big corporations and oil companies but not one penny of tax relief to more than one hundred million Americans? How else could he offer a health care plan that would actually tax people's benefits, or an education plan that would do nothing to help families pay for college, or a plan that would privatize Social Security and gamble your retirement?

It's not because John McCain doesn't care. It's because John McCain doesn't get it.

For over two decades, he's subscribed to that old, discredited Republican philosophy - give more and more to those with the most and hope that prosperity trickles down to everyone else. In Washington, they call this the Ownership Society, but what it really means is - you're on your own. Out of work? Tough luck. No health care? The market will fix it. Born into poverty? Pull yourself up by your own bootstraps - even if you don't have boots. You're on your own.

Well it's time for them to own their failure. It's time for us to change America. You see, we Democrats have a very different measure of what constitutes progress in this country.

We measure progress by how many people can find a job that pays the mortgage; whether you can put a little extra money away at the end of each month so you can someday watch your child receive her college diploma.

We measure progress in the 23 million new jobs that were created when Bill Clinton was President - when the average American family saw its income go up $7,500 instead of down $2,000 like it has under George Bush.

We measure the strength of our economy not by the number of billionaires we have or the profits of the Fortune 500, but by whether someone with a good idea can take a risk and start a new business, or whether the waitress who lives on tips can take a day off to look after a sick child without losing her job - an economy that honors the dignity of work. The fundamentals we use to measure economic strength are whether we are living up to that fundamental promise that has made this country great - a promise that is the only reason I am standing here tonight.

Because in the faces of those young veterans who come back from Iraq and Afghanistan, I see my grandfather, who signed up after Pearl Harbor, marched in Patton's Army, and was rewarded by a grateful nation with the chance to go to college on the GI Bill. In the face of that young student who sleeps just three hours before working the night shift, I think about my mom, who raised my sister and me on her own while she worked and earned her degree; who once turned to food stamps but was still able to send us to the best schools in the country with the help of student loans and scholarships.

When I listen to another worker tell me that his factory has shut down, I remember all those men and women on the South Side of Chicago who I stood by and fought for two decades ago after the local steel plant closed. And when I hear a woman talk about the difficulties of starting her own business, I think about my grandmother, who worked her way up from the secretarial pool to middle-management, despite years of being passed over for promotions because she was a woman. She's the one who taught me about hard work. She's the one who put off buying a new car or a new dress for herself so that I could have a better life. She poured everything she had into me. And although she can no longer travel, I know that she's watching tonight, and that tonight is her night as well.

I don't know what kind of lives John McCain thinks that celebrities lead, but this has been mine. These are my heroes. Theirs are the stories that shaped me. And it is on their behalf that I intend to win this election and keep our promise alive as President of the United States.

What is that promise?

It's a promise that says each of us has the freedom to make of our own lives what we will, but that we also have the obligation to treat each other with dignity and respect. It's a promise that says the market should reward drive and innovation and generate growth, but that businesses should live up to their responsibilities to create American jobs, look out for American workers, and play by the rules of the road.

Ours is a promise that says government cannot solve all our problems, but what it should do is that which we cannot do for ourselves - protect us from harm and provide every child a decent education; keep our water clean and our toys safe; invest in new schools and new roads and new science and technology.

Our government should work for us, not against us. It should help us, not hurt us. It should ensure opportunity not just for those with the most money and influence, but for every American who's willing to work.

That's the promise of America - the idea that we are responsible for ourselves, but that we also rise or fall as one nation; the fundamental belief that I am my brother's keeper; I am my sister's keeper.

That's the promise we need to keep. That's the change we need right now. So let me spell out exactly what that change would mean if I am President.

Change means a tax code that doesn't reward the lobbyists who wrote it, but the American workers and small businesses who deserve it.

Unlike John McCain, I will stop giving tax breaks to corporations that ship jobs overseas, and I will start giving them to companies that create good jobs right here in America.

I will eliminate capital gains taxes for the small businesses and the start-ups that will create the high-wage, high-tech jobs of tomorrow.

I will cut taxes - cut taxes - for 95% of all working families. Because in an economy like this, the last thing we should do is raise taxes on the middle-class. And for the sake of our economy, our security, and the future of our planet, I will set a clear goal as President: in ten years, we will finally end our dependence on oil from the Middle East.

Washington's been talking about our oil addiction for the last thirty years, and John McCain has been there for twenty-six of them. In that time, he's said no to higher fuel-efficiency standards for cars, no to investments in renewable energy, no to renewable fuels. And today, we import triple the amount of oil as the day that Senator McCain took office. Now is the time to end this addiction, and to understand that drilling is a stop-gap measure, not a long-term solution. Not even close.

As President, I will tap our natural gas reserves, invest in clean coal technology, and find ways to safely harness nuclear power. I'll help our auto companies re-tool, so that the fuel-efficient cars of the future are built right here in America. I'll make it easier for the American people to afford these new cars. And I'll invest 150 billion dollars over the next decade in affordable, renewable sources of energy - wind power and solar power and the next generation of biofuels; an investment that will lead to new industries and five million new jobs that pay well and can't ever be outsourced.

America now is not the time for small plans. Now is the time to finally meet our moral obligation to provide every child a world-class education, because it will take nothing less to compete in the global economy. Michelle and I are only here tonight because we were given a chance at an education. And I will not settle for an America where some kids don't have that chance. I'll invest in early childhood education. I'll recruit an army of new teachers, and pay them higher salaries and give them more support. And in exchange, I'll ask for higher standards and more accountability. And we will keep our promise to every young American - if you commit to serving your community or your country, we will make sure you can afford a college education.

Now is the time to finally keep the promise of affordable, accessible health care for every single American. If you have health care, my plan will lower your premiums. If you don't, you'll be able to get the same kind of coverage that members of Congress give themselves. And as someone who watched my mother argue with insurance companies while she lay in bed dying of cancer, I will make certain those companies stop discriminating against those who are sick and need care the most.

Now is the time to help families with paid sick days and better family leave, because nobody in America should have to choose between keeping their jobs and caring for a sick child or ailing parent.

Now is the time to change our bankruptcy laws, so that your pensions are protected ahead of CEO bonuses; and the time to protect Social Security for future generations.

And now is the time to keep the promise of equal pay for an equal day's work, because I want my daughters to have exactly the same opportunities as your sons.

Now, many of these plans will cost money, which is why I've laid out how I'll pay for every dime - by closing corporate loopholes and tax havens that don't help America grow. But I will also go through the federal budget, line by line, eliminating programs that no longer work and making the ones we do need work better and cost less - because we cannot meet twenty-first century challenges with a twentieth century bureaucracy.

And Democrats, we must also admit that fulfilling America's promise will require more than just money. It will require a renewed sense of responsibility from each of us to recover what John F. Kennedy called our "intellectual and moral strength." Yes, government must lead on energy independence, but each of us must do our part to make our homes and businesses more efficient.

Yes, we must provide more ladders to success for young men who fall into lives of crime and despair. But we must also admit that programs alone can't replace parents; that government can't turn off the television and make a child do her homework; that fathers must take more responsibility for providing the love and guidance their children need.

Individual responsibility and mutual responsibility - that's the essence of America's promise. And just as we keep our keep our promise to the next generation here at home, so must we keep America's promise abroad. If John McCain wants to have a debate about who has the temperament, and judgment, to serve as the next Commander-in-Chief, that's a debate I'm ready to have.

For a while Senator McCain was turning his sights to Iraq just days after 9/11, I stood up and opposed this war, knowing that it would distract us from the real threats we face.

When John McCain said we could just "muddle through" in Afghanistan, I argued for more resources and more troops to finish the fight against the terrorists who actually attacked us on 9/11, and made clear that we must take out Osama bin Laden and his lieutenants if we have them in our sights. John McCain likes to say that he'll follow bin Laden to the Gates of Hell - but he won't even go to the cave where he lives.

And today, as my call for a time frame to remove our troops from Iraq has been echoed by the Iraqi government and even the Bush Administration, even after we learned that Iraq has a $79 billion surplus while we're wallowing in deficits, John McCain stands alone in his stubborn refusal to end a misguided war.

That's not the judgment we need. That won't keep America safe. We need a President who can face the threats of the future, not keep grasping at the ideas of the past. You don't defeat a terrorist network that operates in eighty countries by occupying Iraq. You don't protect Israel and deter Iran just by talking tough in Washington.

You can't truly stand up for Georgia when you've strained our oldest alliances. If John McCain wants to follow George Bush with more tough talk and bad strategy, that is his choice - but it is not the change we need.

We are the party of Roosevelt. We are the party of Kennedy. So don't tell me that Democrats won't defend this country. Don't tell me that Democrats won't keep us safe. The Bush-McCain foreign policy has squandered the legacy that generations of Americans -- Democrats and Republicans - have built, and we are here to restore that legacy. As Commander-in-Chief, I will never hesitate to defend this nation, but I will only send our troops into harm's way with a clear mission and a sacred commitment to give them the equipment they need in battle and the care and benefits they deserve when they come home.

I will end this war in Iraq responsibly, and finish the fight against al Qaeda and the Taliban in Afghanistan. I will rebuild our military to meet future conflicts. But I will also renew the tough, direct diplomacy that can prevent Iran from obtaining nuclear weapons and curb Russian aggression. I will build new partnerships to defeat the threats of the 21st century: terrorism and nuclear proliferation; poverty and genocide; climate change and disease. And I will restore our moral standing, so that America is once again that last, best hope for all who are called to the cause of freedom, who long for lives of peace, and who yearn for a better future.

These are the policies I will pursue. And in the weeks ahead, I look forward to debating them with John McCain.

But what I will not do is suggest that the Senator takes his positions for political purposes. Because one of the things that we have to change in our politics is the idea that people cannot disagree without challenging each other's character and patriotism.

The times are too serious; the stakes are too high for this same partisan playbook. So let us agree that patriotism has no party. I love this country, and so do you, and so does John McCain. The men and women who serve in our battlefields may be Democrats and Republicans and Independents, but they have fought together and bled together and some died together under the same proud flag. They have not served a Red America or a Blue America - they have served the United States of America.

So I've got news for you, John McCain. We all put our country first.

America, our work will not be easy. The challenges we face require tough choices, and Democrats as well as Republicans will need to cast off the worn-out ideas and politics of the past. For part of what has been lost these past eight years can't just be measured by lost wages or bigger trade deficits. What has also been lost is our sense of common purpose - our sense of higher purpose. And that's what we have to restore. We may not agree on abortion, but surely we can agree on reducing the number of unwanted pregnancies in this country.

The reality of gun ownership may be different for hunters in rural Ohio than for those plagued by gang-violence in Cleveland, but don't tell me we can't uphold the Second Amendment while keeping AK-47s out of the hands of criminals. I know there are differences on same-sex marriage, but surely we can agree that our gay and lesbian brothers and sisters deserve to visit the person they love in the hospital and to live lives free of discrimination.

Passions fly on immigration, but I don't know anyone who benefits when a mother is separated from her infant child or an employer undercuts American wages by hiring illegal workers. This too is part of America's promise - the promise of a democracy where we can find the strength and grace to bridge divides and unite in common effort. I know there are those who dismiss such beliefs as happy talk. They claim that our insistence on something larger, something firmer and more honest in our public life is just a Trojan Horse for higher taxes and the abandonment of traditional values. And that's to be expected. Because if you don't have any fresh ideas, then you use stale tactics to scare the voters. If you don't have a record to run on, then you paint your opponent as someone people should run from. You make a big election about small things.

And you know what - it's worked before. Because it feeds into the cynicism we all have about government. When Washington doesn't work, all its promises seem empty. If your hopes have been dashed again and again, then it's best to stop hoping, and settle for what you already know.

I get it. I realize that I am not the likeliest candidate for this office. I don't fit the typical pedigree, and I haven't spent my career in the halls of Washington. But I stand before you tonight because all across America something is stirring. What the nay-sayers don't understand is that this election has never been about me. It's been about you.

For eighteen long months, you have stood up, one by one, and said enough to the politics of the past. You understand that in this election, the greatest risk we can take is to try the same old politics with the same old players and expect a different result. You have shown what history teaches us - that at defining moments like this one, the change we need doesn't come from Washington. Change comes to Washington. Change happens because the American people demand it - because they rise up and insist on new ideas and new leadership, a new politics for a new time.

America, this is one of those moments. I believe that as hard as it will be, the change we need is coming. Because I've seen it. Because I've lived it. I've seen it in Illinois, when we provided health care to more children and moved more families from welfare to work. I've seen it in Washington, when we worked across party lines to open up government and hold lobbyists more accountable, to give better care for our veterans and keep nuclear weapons out of terrorist hands. And I've seen it in this campaign. In the young people who voted for the first time, and in those who got involved again after a very long time. In the Republicans who never thought they'd pick up a Democratic ballot, but did. I've seen it in the workers who would rather cut their hours back a day than see their friends lose their jobs, in the soldiers who re-enlist after losing a limb, in the good neighbors who take a stranger in when a hurricane strikes and the floodwaters rise.

This country of ours has more wealth than any nation, but that's not what makes us rich. We have the most powerful military on Earth, but that's not what makes us strong. Our universities and our culture are the envy of the world, but that's not what keeps the world coming to our shores.

Instead, it is that American spirit - that American promise - that pushes us forward even when the path is uncertain; that binds us together in spite of our differences; that makes us fix our eye not on what is seen, but what is unseen, that better place around the bend. That promise is our greatest inheritance. It's a promise I make to my daughters when I tuck them in at night, and a promise that you make to yours - a promise that has led immigrants to cross oceans and pioneers to travel west; a promise that led workers to picket lines, and women to reach for the ballot.

And it is that promise that forty five years ago today, brought Americans from every corner of this land to stand together on a Mall in Washington, before Lincoln's Memorial, and hear a young preacher from Georgia speak of his dream. The men and women who gathered there could've heard many things. They could've heard words of anger and discord. They could've been told to succumb to the fear and frustration of so many dreams deferred. But what the people heard instead - people of every creed and color, from every walk of life - is that in America, our destiny is inextricably linked. That together, our dreams can be one.

"We cannot walk alone," the preacher cried." And as we walk, we must make the pledge that we shall always march ahead. We cannot turn back." America, we cannot turn back. Not with so much work to be done. Not with so many children to educate, and so many veterans to care for. Not with an economy to fix and cities to rebuild and farms to save. Not with so many families to protect and so many lives to mend. America, we cannot turn back. We cannot walk alone. At this moment, in this election, we must pledge once more to march into the future. Let us keep that promise - that American promise - and in the words of Scripture hold firmly, without wavering, to the hope that we confess.

Thank you, God Bless you, and God Bless the United States of America. –Barack Obama"

This speech echoed around the world just as quickly as in this great nation of ours. With both criticism and admiration by many; the truth be told was a huge turning point for many in their decisive vote. Although I had already made up my mind, it did reinforce that decision. I know it is easier said than done, but nonetheless we must push forward and not faint; we will prevail.

Chapter Two

THE START OF A DREAM

Obama's parents met while attending the University of Hawaii at Manoa, where his father was a foreign student. His parents separated when he was only two years old. Obama's father returned to Kenya and saw him only once more before dying in an automobile accident. After the divorce, his mother Dunham married Lolo Soetoro, and moved to Soetoro's home country of Indonesia, where Obama stayed until he was ten years old. He then returned to Honolulu to live with his maternal grandparents. Obama's mother returned to Hawaii in 1972 for several years and then returned back to Indonesia. Obama's mother died of cancer in 1995.

Following high school, Obama moved to Los Angeles, where he studied at Occidental College. He then transferred to Columbia University in New York City, where he majored in political science with a specialization in international relations. Obama graduated with a B.A. from Columbia in 1983, then worked for a year at the Business International Corporation and then at the New York Public Interest Research Group.

Obama attended Harvard Law School in 1988 and at the end of his first year was selected as an editor of the Harvard Law Review. Due to the publicity from his election as the first black president of the Harvard Law Review, he received a contract to write a book about race relations. He originally planned to finish the book in one year, but it took much longer as the book turned into a personal memoir. In order to work without interruptions, Obama and his wife, traveled to Bali where he finished his book. The manuscript was finally published as Dreams from My Father in 1995.

Barack Obama's Illinois State Senate career stretched from 1996 to 2004. Obama also taught constitutional law at the University of Chicago Law School, he was a

Lecturer from 1992 to 1996 and as a Senior Lecturer from 1996-2004, after he was elected to the U.S. Senate.

Obama was sworn in as a senator on January 4, 2005. Obama became the fifth African American Senator in U.S. history. He is the only Senate member of the Congressional Black Caucus.

In a speech at WASHINGTON, D.C. - U.S. Senator Barack Obama (Democrat from Illinois) delivered the following remarks on the Senate floor in support of the Honest Government and Leadership Act. This legislation would provide increased visibility and accountability, reduce the influence of lobbyists and special interests groups, and bring about the much needed changes in Washington. In January, Obama also joined with Senator Russ Feingold (D-WI) to introduce the Lobbying and Ethics Reform Act.

Obama also sponsored an amendment to the Honest Government and Open Leadership Act that required the disclosure of lobbyists that bundle campaign contributions for candidates.

OBAMA:

"First, let me commend Senator Reid for his leadership on this bill and especially my good friend Senator Feingold, who I have worked closely with on this issue over the past year and a half. The bill that's before us today could not be more urgently needed. For too long, the American people have seen lobbyists treat the legislative process like a game, using targeted contributions to maximize their leverage. For too long, people have felt like their voice and their interests have been drowning in a sea of lobbyist money in Washington.

This is not the first time we have faced a crisis of confidence in government. Around the turn of the last century, wealth was becoming more concentrated in the hands of a few robber barons, railroad tycoons and oil magnates. It was an era known as the Gilded Age, and it was made possible by a government that played along.

But when President Theodore Roosevelt took office, he wouldn't play along. He devoted his presidency to busting trusts, breaking up monopolies, and doing his best to give the American people a shot at the American dream once more. America needs this kind of leadership more than ever. We need leadership that sees government not as a tool to enrich well-connected friends and high-priced lobbyists, but as the defender of fairness and opportunity for every American.

We cannot settle for a second Gilded Age in America. And yet we find ourselves once more in the midst of a new economy where more wealth is in danger of falling into fewer hands; where CEO pay grows from year to year as the average worker's pay remains stagnant; where Americans are struggling like never before to pay their medical bills, or their kids' tuition, or high gas prices, all while the profits of the drug and insurance and oil industries have never been higher.

And once again, we are faced with a politics that makes all of this possible. In recent years, the doors of Congress and the White House have been thrown wide open to an army of Washington lobbyists who have turned our government into a game only they can afford to play. Year after year after year, they stand in the way of our progress as a country. They stop us from addressing the issues that matter most to our people.

Take health care. The drug and insurance industries spent $1 billion in lobbying over the last decade. They got what they paid for when their friends in Congress broke the rules and twisted arms to push through a prescription drug bill that actually made it illegal for our own government to negotiate with the pharmaceutical companies for cheaper drug prices. And because reform has been blocked up to now, there are parents and grandparents in this country who are walking into a drugstore and wondering how their Social Security check is going to cover a prescription that's more expensive than it was a month ago; those who are being forced to choose between their medicine and their groceries because they can no longer afford both.

Let me be clear, I do not begrudge businesses for trying to make a profit, and I do not begrudge them for hiring lobbyists to plead their case before Congress. It is protected political speech, and we appreciate that there are many lobbyists who represent their clients well and fairly. But it's time we had a Congress that tells the drug companies and the oil companies and the insurance industry that while they may get a seat at the table in Washington, they don't get to buy every chair.

We need to put an end to the prevailing culture in this town. And that's what we've been trying to do for the past couple of years. Last year, Congress came up with a watered-down version of reform. Last year, I and Senator Feingold and Senator McCain, voted against it because we thought we could do better. So in January, I came back with Senator Feingold and we set a high bar for reform. And I'm pleased to report that the bill before us today comes very close to what we proposed.

By passing this bill, we will ban gifts and meals and end subsidized travel on corporate jets. We will close the revolving door between Pennsylvania Avenue and K Street. And we will make sure that the American people could see all the pet projects that lawmakers are trying to pass before they are actually voted on.

And we'll do something more. Over the objections of powerful voices in both parties, we'll ensure that our laws shine a bright light on how lobbyists help fill the campaign coffers of members of Congress by bundling contributions from others. Because in an era in which soft money is prohibited, the real measure of a lobbyist's influence isn't how much money he's contributed, it's how much he's raised from others.

For too long, this practice has been hidden from public view. But today, we can change that. I'm pleased that the amendment I've offered on bundling is part of this bill, and I want to thank Rep. Chris Van Hollen who has fought so hard to get this provision included in the House bill. As the Washington Post described the bundling provision earlier this year: 'No single change would add more to public understanding of how money really operates in Washington.'

So there's a lot of good in this bill, and I truly hope and believe that it will change the way we do business in Washington. Let's not forget that there's more we need to do.

"One of the things I've argued is the necessity of an independent entity to enforce ethics rules in Congress. Because no matter how well we police our own conduct, so long as we're our own prosecutor, judge, and jury, the public will never have complete trust in our decisions. So far, that's a fight I've lost, but I'll continue to support independent enforcement because I believe it's in our nation's best interests.

I also believe that if we're serious about change, we need to have a real discussion about public financing for congressional elections. Because even if we can stop lobbyists from buying us lunch or taking us out on junkets, they'll still be able to attend our fundraisers - and that's access the average American doesn't have.

In our democracy, the price of access and influence should be nothing more than your voice and your vote. That should be enough for health care reform. That should be enough for a real energy policy. That should be enough to ensure that our government is still the defender of fairness and opportunity for every American.

It's time to show the American people that we have the courage to <u>change</u> the prevailing culture in this city. It's time to give people confidence in their government again. And we have the chance to start doing that with this bill. So I proudly support this legislation."

—Barack Obama

I especially like the part where says: "In our democracy, the price of access and influence should be nothing more than your voice and your vote. That should be enough for health care reform. That should be enough for a real energy policy. That should be enough to ensure that our government is still the defender of fairness and opportunity for every American." but this can only happen with your Vote as an American, we have the power to bring True Change!

Chapter Three

IMMIGRATION REFORM

U.S. Senator Barack Obama delivered the following statement on the Senate floor on an amendment to the immigration reform bill he introduced with Senators Menendez and Feingold.

BARACK:

"I come to the floor tonight to speak about the new 'points' system created in this bill – a proposal that will radically change the way that we judge who is worthy of lawful entry into American society. For decades, American citizens and legal permanent residents have been able to sponsor their family members for entry into our country. For decades, American businesses have been able to sponsor valued employees. The bill before us changes a policy that, while imperfect, has worked well and will replace it with a new, untested, unexamined system to provide visas to immigrants who look good on paper, but who may not have any familial or economic ties to our country.

I have serious concerns about this new experiment in social engineering, not only because of the lack of evidence that it will work, but because the bill says that the new points system cannot be changed for fourteen years. For that reason, I come to the floor today, joined by Senators Menendez and Feingold, to offer amendment 1202 to sunset the points system after five years. I am pleased that immigration experts, religious organizations, and immigrant advocacy organizations have all endorsed our amendment.

These groups have endorsed my amendment because the points system in this bill constitutes a radical shift in immigration policy, premised on the view that there is something wrong with family and employer sponsored immigration. If this program were merely supplementing the current system rather then significantly replacing it, it would not have caused as much concern.

Religious organizations and immigrant advocacy groups also have endorsed my amendment because the decisions about what characteristics are deserving of points -- and how points are allocated for those characteristics -- were made without a single hearing or public examination."

And they support the amendment because the new points system shifts us too far away from the value we place on family ties and moves us toward a class-based immigration system where some people are welcome only as guest workers, but never as full participants in our democracy. Indeed, the practical effect of the points system is to make it more difficult for Americans and legal permanent residents with family living in Latin America to bring them here.

Our current immigration system delivers the lion's share of green cards – about 63% -- to family members of Americans and legal permanent residents, while roughly 16% of visas are allocated to employment-based categories. The bill before us would reduce visas allocated to the family system in order to dramatically increase the proportion of visas distributed based on economic "points." Once implemented, these new economic points' visas would then account for about 40% of all visas, while family visas would account for less than half of all visas, with the remainder going for humanitarian purposes.

Under the new system, just a few of the current family preferences would be retained in any recognizable form. Spouses and children of U.S. citizens would still be able to come. However, parents of U.S. citizens would no longer be counted as immediate families, and thus most parents seeking to join their children and grandchildren in the United States would be denied green cards. The rest of the current family preferences – siblings, adult children, and many parents -- would be eviscerated.

The new points system also would eliminate employment-based green cards altogether, forcing employers recruiting workers abroad to rely exclusively on short-term H-1B and Y visas. This proposal takes an admittedly problematic, employment-based visa system and replaces it with a far more problematic, temporary worker program. The design of the points system leaves numerous questions unanswered. Beyond pushing workers from Latin America to the back of an endless line, with no hope of ever reaching the front, the new points system leaves unspecified the crucial question of how migrants with sufficient points will be prioritized. Government bureaucrats would thus be left with unprecedented discretion to determine which immigrants have acceptable education, employment history, and work experience to merit admission into the country.

Taken together, the questionable design of this points program and the fundamental shift away from family preferences in the allocation of visas raise enough red flags that we should not simply rubber stamp this proposal and allow it to go forward.

Let me be clear: Senators Menendez, Feingold, and I are not proposing to strike the program from the bill. But this system should be revisited after a reasonable amount of time to determine whether it's working, how it can be improved, and whether we should return to the current family and employer based system that has worked so well.

We live in a global economy, and I do believe that America will be strengthened if we welcome more immigrants who have mastered science and engineering. But, we cannot weaken the very essence of what America is by turning our backs on immigrants who want to reunite with their family members, or immigrants who have a willingness to work hard but who may not have the right graduate degrees.

This is not who we are as a country. Should those without graduate degrees who spoke Italian or Polish or German, instead of English, have been turned back at Ellis Island? Should the immigrants from Asia who arrived at Angel Island to build our railroads have been told that they could only come for two years because they had no hope of passing a points test? How many of our ancestors would have been allowed to enter the U.S. under this new system?

Character and work ethic have long defined generations of immigrants to America. But these qualities are beyond the scope of this bill's points system. It tells us nothing about what people who have been without opportunity can achieve once they are here. It tells us nothing about the potential of their children to serve and to lead.

We are Americans. We do not have a caste or class based society, and we do not need a caste or class based immigration system.

In short, the points system raises some serious concerns for me. Now, I'm willing to defer to those senators who negotiated this provision and say we should give this a try.

But I'm not willing to say that this untested system should be made virtually permanent. For that reason, I urge my colleagues to support this common-sense amendment to sunset this points system after five years so we can examine its effectiveness and necessity." – Barack Obama

Senator Obama's Statement on Latin America:

"Mr. OBAMA. Mr. President, later today, President Bush will start on a six day visit to five countries in the Western Hemisphere – Brazil, Uruguay, Colombia, Guatemala, and Mexico. The trip comes at an important time for the region, and for U.S. relations with our hemispheric neighbors. In an historic convergence, during a 13 month period beginning in November, 2005, and ending this past December, a dozen countries throughout Latin America and the Caribbean held presidential elections.

Those elections are a testament to the tremendous democratic strides made throughout the Americas during the past two decades, and saw governments elected to power that span the ideological spectrum.

In many ways, the election results symbolize the important political, economic, and social change occurring throughout the Americas. As many have noted, the elections gave voice to a yearning across the hemisphere for social and economic development – a yearning among tens of millions of people for a better life. This is a welcome development, and a challenge to all of us who wish to see the Americas continue down a path of democracy with justice. Because while we should welcome this democratic call for change, we must recognize that hard and steady work lies ahead to make these hopes a reality.

That a desire for fundamental change has been expressed through the ballot box is an enormous stride forward. Too often, change in the Americas has occurred in an anti-democratic fashion. Those days must permanently be put to rest. All citizens of the Americas have a fundamental right to live in freedom, and to express themselves through robust democratic institutions.

That a desire for expanded prosperity has been given such clear voice raises the stakes. Governments must now do more to address the basic needs and aspirations of their people in an effective, democratic, and sustainable way. A failure to fulfill the most basic functions of government, and a failure to create the conditions in which tens of millions across the Americas can realize their hopes and break free of poverty could undo these gains. The denial of opportunity is now the most significant threat to the consolidation of democracy in the region.

Unfortunately, the elections and this desire for change have occurred at a time when U.S. prestige and influence have fallen to depths not seen in at least a generation. As has been the case throughout the world, our standing in the Americas has suffered as a result of the misguided policies and actions of the Bush Administration. It will take significant work to repair the damage wrought by six years of neglect and mismanagement of relations.

The United States can ill afford this deterioration of our standing. With each passing day, we draw closer together to our neighbors to the south. This convergence creates new challenges, but it also opens the door to a more hopeful future. If we pay careful attention to developments throughout the region, and respond to them in a thoughtful and respectful way, then we can advance our many and varied national interests at stake in the Americas.

I welcome the President's decision to travel to five important countries in Latin America, and to reaffirm the importance of our relationship with the more than 500 million people who live to our south. I am, however, disappointed that the President has fallen so short in his promise to transform U.S. relations with the Americas.

Our regional relationships cannot be properly attended to with one six-day trip, a series of photo opportunities, and some lofty rhetoric on collaboration. Nor does the Bush Administration's declaration of 2007 as the year of engagement with the Americas suffice. One year of engagement out of seven is simply not good enough. In light of the Bush Administration's woeful record, creating false expectations does more harm than good.

We must be realistic about the challenges we face, and what we are doing to address them. We must devote our full time, and our respectful attention to our relations within the hemisphere.

Earlier this week, President Bush spoke of a "social justice" agenda for the Americas. He was right to underscore the importance of addressing the basic needs of millions of our neighbors languishing in poverty. The primary responsibility for doing so, of course, lies with the governments and societies throughout the hemisphere. Yet helping to lift people out of widespread poverty is in our interests, just as it is in accord with our values.

When instability spreads to our south, our security and economic interests are at risk. When our neighbors suffer, all of the Americas suffer.

The United States has an important role to play. Yet the President sends a mixed message when he makes his call for a social justice agenda after presenting the Congress with a budget for fiscal year 2008 that, with the exception of HIV/AIDS funding, slashes both assistance for economic development and health programs in the Americas. At a time when our standing in the hemisphere is so low, we cannot afford to send this kind of message. Our commitment to justice in the Americas must be expressed in more than one thoughtful expression in one pre-trip speech. Our commitment must be matched by our deeds, not just our words.

It is my hope that the President will break from his practice of touting the importance of the Americas during his travels only to turn his back upon his return.

Each stop on the President's trip presents an opportunity to move beyond rhetoric, to renew relations in the hemisphere, and to set a new course for sustained follow-through in a way that advances important U.S. interests.

In Brazil, it has been reported that President Bush is expected to join with President Luiz Inacio Lula de Silva to announce greater ethanol cooperation between the United States and Brazil. Together, the United States and Brazil are the world's largest ethanol producers and consumers. Brazil's more than 30 years of renewable fuel technology investments allowed it to achieve energy independence last year. Ethanol now accounts for 40 percent of Brazil's fuel usage. More than 80 percent of cars sold in Brazil today are flex fuel vehicles—capable of running on gasoline, ethanol, or a mixture thereof.

Greater Brazilian production of renewable fuels could boost sustainable economic development throughout Latin America, and reshape the geopolitics of energy in the hemisphere, reducing the oil-driven influence of Venezuela's Hugo Chavez. The more inter-hemispheric production and use of ethanol and other biofuels occurs, and the more such indigenously-produced renewable fuels are used to replace fossil fuels, the better it is for our friends in the hemisphere.

As it relates to our country's drive toward energy independence, it does not serve our national and economic security to replace imported oil with Brazilian ethanol. In other words, those who advocate replacement of US-based biofuels production with Brazilian ethanol exports however well intentioned they may be, are both misunderstanding our long term energy security challenge and ignoring a valuable foreign policy opportunity. The U.S. needs to dramatically expand domestic biofuels production, not embrace a short term fix that discourages investment in the expansion of the domestic renewable fuels in industry. Also, accelerating technology advances and transferring the technology to our neighbors in the Caribbean and South America will help them employ their own resources to produce environmentally clean ethanol to reduce their imported oil bill, thereby promoting economic stability in the Caribbean and South and Central America and strengthen the U.S.-Brazil relationship.

Mr. President, it is vital that President Bush keeps the Congress involved each step forward in a U.S.-Brazil relationship based on renewable fuels. This relationship must be structured so as not to hamper the domestic production of renewable fuels or the development of new technologies here at home that can enhance our energy security.

In Uruguay, President Bush has the opportunity to forge closer ties with President Tabaré Vázquez, and to show that the United States is ready, willing, and able to work productively with democratic-left governments. That this ability is in question and that it requires explaining underscores how badly the President and his administration have misunderstood and mismanaged the political, economic, and social change occurring throughout the Americas. The United States is seen as supporting democracy when it produces a desired result.

It is vital to reverse that trend. I hope the President can begin that process, even if we have a long way to go.

The United States has invested a great deal—nearly $5 billion during the past 7 years—to help stabilize Colombia. A more peaceful, just, and stable Colombia is undoubtedly in our national interest. It is imperative; however, that greater peace and stability contribute to a reduction in the flow of drugs from Colombia to the United States. Thus far, we have not seen the kind of drop off that the effective pursuit of our interests demands.

President Bush's closest ally in the region—Colombian President Alvaro Uribe—is embroiled in a controversy that has led to the arrest of eight of his supporters in the Colombian Congress and his former confidant and former chief of Colombia's secret police for ties to the country's narco-terrorist paramilitaries.

President Bush must be careful to keep the pursuit of U.S. interests in Colombia distinct from specific personalities, or personal relationships. The further consolidation of legitimate governing institutions in

Colombia – and the extension of their reach throughout Colombia – are clearly in the national interest of the United States, and the interest of Colombia.

Guatemala shares deep connections with the United States. Nearly one in ten Guatemalans now lives in the United States. Nearly $3 billion were remitted from the United States to Guatemala in 2005, representing approximately 10 percent of that country's Gross Domestic Product. Having emerged from decades of internal conflict that left as many as 200,000 of its citizens dead, Guatemala finds itself struggling with a new scourge of violence that is causing instability. Gang and drug-related criminal violence and the country's staggering levels of poverty pose enormous challenges— challenges that affect our country as well. I am encouraged to see the Bush Administration's new commitment to supporting a Central American regional approach to combat transnational gangs. This initiative should incorporate the most effective techniques and practices from the United States and from throughout the region. The United States must take the lead in rolling back the detrimental influence of these gangs in our own society, and in Central America.

The relationship between the United States and Mexico is among our most important in the world. Getting it right is vital to advancing our core economic and security interests. To do that, a great deal of work needs to be done. Mexico is making strong efforts to address the drug trade, and is working cooperatively with the United States on a number of security issues. But our complex relationship with Mexico has become captive to a single issue: the immigration debate in our country.

There is consensus that our immigration system is broken. It is past time to fix it, and I am proud of my own support for a workable solution. We need comprehensive approach to illegal immigration that stops the flow of illegal immigrants across our borders, better manages immigration flows going forward, and deals fairly with the illegal immigrants already living and working in our country.

A workable solution will require bipartisan support and I will work to build it. The President has consistently voiced his support for comprehensive immigration reform. It is my hope that upon his return from Mexico he will get to work, converting his words into deeds to help push comprehensive immigration reform forward.

Mr. President a great deal of work needs to be done. We need to restore U.S. relations in the hemisphere. We need to consolidate the gains that have been made in the sweeping change of the last few years. We need to sustain our commitment to democracy, to social justice, and to opportunity for our neighbors to the south. The western hemisphere is too important to our core economic and security interests to be treated with the neglect and mismanagement that have defined the past six years.

It is my hope that President Bush's trip marks the opening of a new chapter of cooperation and partnership – a chapter of partnership with our neighbors to promote democracy with social and economic development for the benefit of all of us who live in the Americas. It is time for the United States to reclaim and renew its historic role as a leader in the hemisphere, and an example of hope for all who seek opportunity in the Americas.

I thank the President and I yield the floor." —Barack Obama.

I live in a border town near South Texas and Mexico, and see first hand the illegal smuggling of drugs, human trafficking; we need change in America.

Chapter Four

HEALTH CARE

In a Families USA Conference held in Washington, DC, Barack made the following speech:

"Thank you Ron Pollack and thank you Families USA for inviting me to speak here this morning.

On this January morning of two thousand and seven, more than sixty years after President Truman first issued the call for national health insurance, we find ourselves in the midst of an historic moment on health care.

From Maine to California, from business to labor, from Democrats to Republicans, the emergence of new and bold proposals from across the spectrum has effectively ended the debate over whether or not we should have universal health care in this country.

Plans that tinker and halfway measures now belong to yesterday. The President's latest proposal that does little to bring down cost or guarantee coverage falls into this category.

There will be many others offered in the coming campaign, and I am working with experts to develop my own plan as we speak, but let's make one thing clear right here, right now: In the 2008 campaign, affordable, universal health care for every single American must not be a question of whether, it must be a question of how. We have the ideas, we have the resources, and we will have universal health care in this country by the end of the next president's first term.

I know there's a cynicism out there about whether this can happen, and there's reason for it. Every four years, health care plans are offered up in campaigns with great fanfare and promise. But once those campaigns end, the plans collapse under the weight of Washington politics, leaving the rest of America to struggle with skyrocketing costs.

For too long, this debate has been stunted by what I call the smallness of our politics - the idea that there isn't much we can agree on or do about the major challenges facing our country.

And when some try to propose something bold, the interests groups and the partisans treat it like a sporting event, with each side keeping score of whose up and who's down, using fear and divisiveness and other cheap tricks to win their argument, even if we lose our solution in the process.

Well we can't afford another disappointing charade in 2008. It's not only tiresome, it's wrong. Wrong when businesses have to layoff one employee because they can't afford the health care of another. Wrong when a parent cannot take a sick child to the doctor because they cannot afford the bill that comes with it. Wrong when 46 million Americans have no health care at all.

In a country that spends more on health care than any other nation on Earth, it's just wrong. And yet, in recent years, what's caught the attention of those who haven't always been in favor of reform is the realization that this crisis isn't just morally offensive, it's economically untenable.

For years, the can't-do crowd has scared the American people into believing that universal health care would mean socialized medicine and burdensome taxes - that we should just stay out of the way and tinker at the margins. You know the statistics. Family premiums are up by nearly 87% over the last five years, growing five times faster than workers' wages.

Deductibles are up 50%. Co-payments for care and prescriptions are through the roof. Nearly 11 million Americans who are already insured spent more than a quarter of their salary on health care last year. And over half of all family bankruptcies today are caused by medical bills. But they say it's too costly to act. Almost half of all small businesses no longer offer health care to their workers, and so many others have responded to rising costs by laying off workers or shutting their doors for good.

Some of the biggest corporations in America, giants of industry like GM and Ford, are watching foreign competitors based in countries with universal health care run circles around them, with a GM car containing twice as much health care cost as a Japanese car. But they say it's too risky to act. They tell us it's too expensive to cover the uninsured, but they don't mention that every time an American without health insurance walks into an emergency room, we pay even more.

Our family's premiums are $922 higher because of the cost of care for the uninsured.

We pay $15 billion more in taxes because of the cost of care for the uninsured. And it's trapped us in a vicious cycle. As the uninsured cause premiums to rise, more employers drop coverage. As more employers drop coverage, more people become uninsured, and premiums rise even further.

But the skeptics tell us that reform is too costly, too risky, and too impossible for America. Well the skeptics must be living somewhere else. Because when you see what the health care crisis is doing to our families, to our economy, to our country, you realize that caution is what's costly. Inaction is what's risky. Doing nothing is what's impossible when it comes to health care in America.

It's time to act. This isn't a problem of money; this is a problem of will. A failure of leadership. We already spend $2.2 trillion a year on health care in this country. My colleague, Senator Ron Wyden, who's recently developed a bold new health care plan of his own, tells it this way: For the money Americans spent on health care last year, we could have hired a group of skilled physicians, paid each one of them $200,000 to care for just seven families, and guaranteed every single American quality, affordable health care.

So where's all that money going? We know that a quarter of it - one out of every four health care dollars - is spent on non-medical costs; mostly bills and paperwork. And we also know that this is completely unnecessary. Almost every other industry in the world has saved billions on these administrative costs by doing it all online. Every transaction you make at a bank now costs them less than a penny. Even at the Veterans Administration, where it used to cost nine dollars to pull up your medical record, new technology means you can call up the same record on the internet for next to nothing.

But because we haven't updated technology in the rest of the health care industry, a single transaction still costs up to twenty-five dollars - not one dime of which goes toward improving the quality of our health care. This is simply inexcusable, and if we brought our entire health care system online, something everyone from Ted Kennedy to Newt Gingrich believes we should do, we'd already be saving over $600 million a year on health care costs.

The federal government should be leading the way here. If you do business with the federal employee health benefits program, you should move to an electronic claims system. If you are a provider who works with

Medicare, you should have to report your patient's health outcomes, so that we can figure out, on a national level, how to improve health care quality. These are all things experts tell us must be done but aren't being done. And the federal government should lead.

Another, more controversial area we need to look at is how much of our health care spending is going toward the record-breaking profits earned by the drug and health care industry. It's perfectly understandable for a corporation to try and make a profit, but when those profits are soaring higher and higher each year while millions lose their coverage and premiums skyrocket, we have a responsibility to ask why.

At a time when businesses are facing increased competition and workers rarely stay with one company throughout their lives, we also have to ask if the employer-based system of health care itself is still the best for providing insurance to all Americans. We have to ask what we can do to provide more Americans with preventative care, which would mean fewer doctor's visits and less cost down the road. We should make sure that every single child who's eligible is signed up for the children's health insurance program, and the federal government should make sure that our states have the money to make that happen.

And we have to start looking at some of the interesting ideas on comprehensive reform that are coming out of states like Maine and Illinois and California, to see what we can replicate on a national scale and what will move us toward that goal of universal coverage for all.

But regardless of what combination of policies and proposals get us to this goal, we must reach it. We must act. And we must act boldly. As one health care advocate recently said, "The most expensive course is to do nothing." But it wasn't a liberal Democrat or union leader who said this.

It was the president of the very health industry association that funded the "Harry and Louise" ads designed to kill the Clinton health care plan in the early nineties.

The debate in this country over health care has shifted. The support for comprehensive reform that organizations like Families USA have worked so hard to build is now widespread, and the diverse group of business and health industry interests that are part of your Health Care Coverage Coalition is a testament to that success. And so Washington no longer has an excuse for caution. Leaders no longer have a reason to be timid. And America can no longer afford inaction. That's not who we are - and that's not the story of our nation's improbable progress.

Half a century ago, America found itself in the midst of another health care crisis. For millions of elderly Americans, the single greatest cause of poverty and hardship was the crippling cost of health care and the lack of affordable insurance. Two out of every three elderly Americans had annual incomes of less than $1,000, and only one in eight had health insurance. As health care and hospital costs continued to rise, more and more private insurers simply refused to insure our elderly, believing they were too great of a risk to care for. The resistance to action was fierce. Proponents of health care reform were opposed by well-financed, well-connected interest groups who spared no expense in telling the American people that these efforts were "dangerous" and "un-American," "revolutionary" and even "deadly."

And yet the reformers marched on. They testified before Congress and they took their case to the country and they introduced dozens of different proposals but always, always they stood firm on their goal to provide health care for every American senior. And finally, after years of advocacy and negotiation and plenty of setbacks, President Lyndon Johnson signed the Medicare bill into law on July 30th of 1965.

The signing ceremony was held in Missouri, in a town called Independence, with the first man who was bold enough to issue the call for universal health care - President Harry Truman. And as he stood with Truman by his side and signed what would become the most successful government program in history - a program that had seemed impossible for so long - President Johnson looked out at the crowd and said, "History shapes men, but it is a necessary faith of leadership that men can help shape history."

Never forget that we have it within our power to shape history in this country. It is not in our character to sit idly by as victims of fate or circumstance, for we are a people of action and innovation, forever pushing the boundaries of what's possible.

Now is the time to push those boundaries once more. We have come so far in the debate on health care in this country, but now we must finally answer the call first issued by Truman, advanced by Johnson, and fought for by so many leaders and Americans throughout the last century. The time has come for universal health care in America. And I look forward to working with all of you to meet this challenge in the weeks and months to come. Thank you."

In the fourth Democratic debate held by CNN, Barack was asked the following question; CNN's MR. COOPER: "Senator Obama, your supporters say you are different. Your critics say you're inexperienced, you're a first-term senator."

SENATOR OBAMA: "Well, I think the questioner hit the nail on the head. As I travel around the country, people have an urgent desire for change in Washington. And we are not going to fix health care, we are not going to fix energy, we are not going to do anything about our education system unless we change how business is done in Washington. Now, part of that is bringing people together, as Chris said, but part of it is also overcoming special interests and lobbyists who are writing legislation that's critical to the American people. And one of the things I bring is a perspective as a community organizer, as a state legislator, as well as a U.S. senator, that says Washington has to change." -Barack Obama.

America, the key issue should be, let's bring change to our politicians in congress; and if we can bring that much needed change to Washington the rest will follow; Barack Promises to bring that change, so please back him up as our next president of the United States.

Chapter Five

RIGHT TO VOTE

Senator Barack Obama's Remarks In Support of H.R. 9, the Voting Rights Act
Thursday, July 20, 2006.

"Mr. President, I rise today, both humbled and honored by the opportunity to express my support for renewal of the expiring provisions of the Voting Rights Act of 1965.

I want to thank the many people inside and outside of Congress who worked so hard over the past year to get us here. We owe a debt of gratitude to the leadership on both sides of the aisle, and we owe special thanks to Chairmen Sensenbrenner and Specter, Ranking Members Conyers and Leahy, and Rep. Mel Watt. Without their work and dedication - and the support of voting rights advocates around the country - I doubt this bill would have come before us so soon.

And I want to thank both chambers, and both sides of the aisle, for getting this done with the same broad support that drove the original Act 40 years ago. At a time when Americans are frustrated with the partisan bickering that too often stalls our work, the refreshing display of bipartisanship we are seeing today reflects our collective belief in the success of the Act and reminds us of how effective we can be when we work together.

Nobody can deny that we've come a long way since 1965.

Look at registration numbers. Only two years after passage of the original Act, registration numbers for minority voters in some states doubled. Soon after, not a single state covered by the Voting Rights Act had registered less than half of its minority voting-age population.

Look at the influence of African-American elected officials at all levels of government. There are African-

American members of Congress. Since 2001, our nation's top diplomat has been an African-American.

In fact, most of America's elected African-American officials come from the states covered by Section 5 of the Voting Rights Act - states like Mississippi and Alabama and Louisiana and Georgia.

But to me, the most striking evidence of our progress can be found right across this building, in my dear friend, Congressman John Lewis, who was on the front lines of the civil rights movement, risking life and limb for freedom. And on March 7, 1965, he led 600 peaceful protestors demanding the right to vote across the Edmund Pettus Bridge in Selma, Alabama.

I've often thought about the people on the Edmund Pettus Bridge that day. Not only John Lewis and Hosea Williams leading the march, but the hundreds of everyday Americans who left their homes and their churches to join it. Blacks and whites, teenagers and children, teachers and bankers and shopkeepers - a beloved community of God's children ready to stand for freedom.

And I wonder, where did they find that kind of courage? When you're facing row after row of state troopers on horseback armed with billy clubs and tear gas...when they're coming toward you spewing hatred and violence, how do you simply stop, kneel down, and pray to the Lord for salvation?

But the most amazing thing of all is that after that day - after John Lewis was beaten within an inch of his life, after people's heads were gashed open and their eyes were burned and they watched their children's innocence literally beaten out of them...after all that, they went back to march again.

They marched again. They crossed the bridge. They awakened a nation's conscience, and not five months later, the Voting Rights Act of 1965 was signed into law. And it was reauthorized in 1970, 1975, and 1982.

Now, in 2006, John Lewis, the physical scars from those marches still visible, is an original cosponsor of the fourth reauthorization of the Voting Rights Act, and he was joined last week by 389 of his House colleagues in voting for its passage.

There are some who argue the Act is no longer needed, that the protections of Section 5's "pre-clearance" requirement - a requirement that ensures certain states are upholding the right to vote - are targeting the wrong states. But the evidence refutes that notion. Of the 1,100 objections issued by the Department of Justice since 1965, 56% occurred since the last reauthorization in 1982. So, despite the progress these states have made in upholding the right to vote, it's clear that problems still exist.

Others have argued against renewing Section 203's protection of language minorities. Unfortunately, these arguments have been tied to the debate over immigration and muddle a non-controversial issue - protecting the right to vote - with one of today's most contentious debates.

But let's remember: you can't request language assistance if you're not a voter, and you can't be a voter if you're not a citizen. And while voters, as citizens, must be proficient in English, many are simply more confident that they can cast ballots printed in their native languages without making errors.

A representative of the Southwestern Voter Registration Project is quoted as saying: "Citizens who prefer Spanish registration cards do so because they feel more connected to the process; they also feel they trust the process more when they understand it." These sentiments - connection to and trust in our democratic process - are exactly what we want from our voting rights legislation.

Our challenges don't end at reauthorizing the Voting Rights Act either. We have to prevent the problems we've seen in recent elections from happening again. We've seen political operatives purge voters from registration rolls for no legitimate reason, prevent eligible ex-felons from casting ballots, distribute polling equipment unevenly, and deceive voters about the time, location and rules of elections. Unfortunately, these efforts have been directed primarily at minorities, the disabled, low-income individuals, and other historically disenfranchised groups.

The Help America Vote Act was a big step in the right direction, but we need to do more. We need to fully fund HAVA. We need to enforce critical requirements like statewide registration databases. We need to make sure polling equipment is distributed equitably and that the equipment works. And we need to work on getting more people to the polls on Election Day.

We need to make sure that minority voters are not the subject of deplorable intimidation tactics when they do get to the polls. In 2004, Native American voters in South Dakota were confronted by men posing as law enforcement. These hired intimidators joked about jail time for ballot missteps, and followed voters to their cars to record their license plate numbers.

In Lake County, Ohio, some voters received a memo on bogus Board of Elections letterhead informing voters who registered through Democratic and NAACP drives that they could not vote.

In Wisconsin, a flier purporting to be from the "Milwaukee Black Voters League" was circulated in predominantly African-American neighborhoods with the following message: "If you've already voted in any election this year, you can't vote in the presidential election. If you violate any of these laws, you can get ten years in prison and your children will get taken away from you."

So, we have much more work to do. This occasion is cause for celebration, but it's also an opportunity to renew our commitment to voting rights. As Congressman Lewis said last week: "It's clear that we have come a great distance, but we still have a great distance to go."

The memory of Selma still lives on in the spirit of the Voting Rights Act. Since that day, the Voting Rights Act has been a critical tool in ensuring that all Americans not only have the right to vote, but the right to have their vote counted. Those of us concerned about protecting those rights can't afford to sit on our laurels upon reauthorization of this bill. We must take advantage of this rare united front and continue the fight to ensure unimpeded access to the polls for all Americans. In other words, we need to take the spirit that existed on that bridge, and we have to spread it across this country.

Two weeks after the first march was turned back, Dr. King told a gathering of organizers and activists and community members that they should not despair because the arc of the moral universe is long, but it bends towards justice. That's because of the work that each of us do to bend it towards justice. It's because of people like John Lewis and Fannie Lou Hamer and Coretta Scott King and Rosa Parks, all the giants upon whose shoulders we stand that we are the beneficiaries of that arc bending towards justice.

That's why I stand here today. I would not be in the United States Senate had it not been for the efforts and courage of so many parents and grandparents and ordinary people who were willing to reach up and bend

that arc in the direction of justice. I hope we continue to see that spirit live on, not just during this debate, but throughout all our work here in the Senate. Thank you."
-Barack Obama.

America, let us bend that arch towards justice; don't let the ignorance of a few misguided followers determine the presidency, please vote.

Chapter Six

DR. KING

The following is Mr. Obama's speech at the Dr. Martin Luther King Jr. National Memorial Groundbreaking Ceremony:

"I want to thank first of all the King family, we would not be here without them, I want to thank Mr. Johnson and the foundation for allowing me to share this day with all of you. I wish to recognize as well my colleagues in the United States Senate who have helped make today possible. Senators Paul Sarbanes and John Warner, who wrote the bill for this memorial. Senators Thad Cochran and Robert Byrd who appropriated the money to help build it. Thank you all.

I have two daughters, ages five and eight. And when I see the plans for this memorial, I think about what it will be like when I first bring them here upon the memorial's completion. I imagine us walking down to this tidal basin, between one memorial dedicated to the man who helped give birth to a nation, and another dedicated to the man who preserved it.

I picture us walking beneath the shadows cast by the Mountain of Despair, and gazing up at the Stone of Hope, and reading the quotes on the wall together as the water falls like rain. And at some point, I know that one of my daughters will ask, perhaps my youngest, will ask, "Daddy, why is this monument here? What did this man do?" How might I answer them? Unlike the others commemorated in this place, Dr. Martin Luther King Jr. was not a president of the United States - at no time in his life did he hold public office.

He was not a hero of foreign wars. He never had much money, and while he lived he was reviled at least as much as he was celebrated. By his own accounts, he was a man frequently racked with doubt, a man not without flaws, a man who, like Moses before him, more than once questioned why he had been chosen for so arduous a task - the task of leading a people to freedom, the task of healing the festering wounds of a nation's original sin.

And yet lead a nation he did. Through words he gave voice to the voiceless. Through deeds he gave courage to the faint of heart. By dint of vision, and determination, and most of all faith in the redeeming power of love, he endured the humiliation of arrest, the loneliness of a prison cell, the constant threats to his life, until he finally inspired a nation to transform itself, and begin to live up to the meaning of its creed.

Like Moses before him, he would never live to see the Promised Land. But from the mountain top, he pointed the way for us - a land no longer torn asunder with racial hatred and ethnic strife, a land that measured itself by how it treats the least of these, a land in which strength is defined not simply by the capacity to wage war but by the determination to forge peace - a land in which all of God's children might come together in a spirit of brotherhood. We have not yet arrived at this longed for place. For all the progress we have made, there are times when the land of our dreams recedes from us - when we are lost, wandering spirits, content with our suspicions and our angers, our long-held grudges and petty disputes, our frantic diversions and tribal allegiances.

And yet, by erecting this monument, we are reminded that this different, better place beckons us, and that we will find it not across distant hills or within some hidden valley, but rather we will find it somewhere in our hearts. In the Book of Micah, Chapter 6, verse 8, the prophet says that God has already told us what is good. "What doth the Lord require of thee, the verse tells us, but to do justly, and to love mercy, and to walk humbly with thy God?"

The man we honor today did what God required. In the end, that is what I will tell my daughters - I will leave it to their teachers and their history books to tell them the rest. As Dr. King asked to be remembered, I will tell them that this man gave his life serving others. I will tell them that this man tried to love somebody.

I will tell them that because he did these things, they live today with the freedom God intended, their citizenship unquestioned, their dreams unbounded. And I will tell them that they too can love. That they too can serve. And that each generation is beckoned anew, to fight for what is right, and strive for what is just, and to find within itself the spirit, the sense of purpose, that can remake a nation and transform a world. Thank you very much." -Barack Obama.

Dr. Martin Luther King's speech given in 1963:

"I am happy to join with you today in what will go down in history as the greatest demonstration for freedom in the history of our nation.

Five score years ago, a great American, in whose symbolic shadow we stand today, signed the Emancipation Proclamation. This momentous decree came as a great beacon light of hope to millions of Negro slaves who had been seared in the flames of withering injustice. It came as a joyous daybreak to end the long night of their captivity.

But 100 years later, the Negro still is not free. One hundred years later, the life of the Negro is still sadly crippled by the manacles of segregation and the chains of discrimination. One hundred years later, the Negro lives on a lonely island of poverty in the midst of a vast ocean of material prosperity. One hundred years later, the Negro is still languished in the corners of American society and finds himself an exile in his own land. And so we've come here today to dramatize a shameful condition.

In a sense we've come to our nation's capital to cash a check. When the architects of our republic wrote the magnificent words of the Constitution and the Declaration of Independence, they were signing a promissory note to which every American was to fall heir. This note was a promise that all men - yes, black men as well as white men - would be guaranteed the unalienable rights of life, liberty, and the pursuit of happiness.

It is obvious today that America has defaulted on this promissory note insofar as her citizens of color are concerned. Instead of honoring this sacred obligation, America has given the Negro people a bad check, a check that has come back marked "insufficient funds."

But we refuse to believe that the bank of justice is bankrupt. We refuse to believe that there are insufficient funds in the great vaults of opportunity of this nation. And so we've come to cash this check, a check that will give us upon demand the riches of freedom and security of justice. We have also come to his hallowed spot to remind America of the fierce urgency of now. This is no time to engage in the luxury of cooling off or to take the tranquilizing drug of gradualism.

Now is the time to make real the promises of democracy. Now is the time to rise from the dark and desolate valley of segregation to the sunlit path of racial justice. Now is the time to lift our nation from the quicksand's of racial injustice to the solid rock of brotherhood. Now is the time to make justice a reality for all of God's children.

It would be fatal for the nation to overlook the urgency of the moment. This sweltering summer of the Negro's legitimate discontent will not pass until there is an invigorating autumn of freedom and equality. Nineteen sixty-three is not an end but a beginning. Those who hoped that the Negro needed to blow off steam and will now be content will have a rude awakening if the nation returns to business as usual. There will be neither rest nor tranquility in America until the Negro is granted his citizenship rights. The whirlwinds of revolt will continue to shake the foundations of our nation until the bright day of justice emerges.

But there is something that I must say to my people who stand on the warm threshold which leads into the palace of justice. In the process of gaining our rightful place we must not be guilty of wrongful deeds. Let us not seek to satisfy our thirst for freedom by drinking from the cup of bitterness and hatred. We must forever conduct our struggle on the high plane of dignity and discipline. We must not allow our creative protest to degenerate into physical violence. Again and again we must rise to the majestic heights of meeting physical force with soul force. The marvelous new militancy which has engulfed the Negro community must not lead us to a distrust of all white people, for many of our white brothers, as evidenced by their presence here today, have come to realize that their destiny is tied up with our destiny. And they have come to realize that their freedom is inextricably bound to our freedom. We cannot walk alone.

And as we walk, we must make the pledge that we shall always march ahead. We cannot turn back. There are those who are asking the devotees of civil rights, "When will you be satisfied?" We can never be satisfied as long as the Negro is the victim of the unspeakable horrors of police brutality. We can never be satisfied as long as our bodies, heavy with the fatigue of travel, cannot gain lodging in the motels of the highways and the hotels of the cities. We cannot be satisfied as long as the Negro's basic mobility is from a smaller ghetto to a larger one. We can never be satisfied as long as our children are stripped of their selfhood and robbed of their dignity by signs stating "for whites only." We cannot be satisfied as long as a Negro in Mississippi cannot vote and a Negro in New York believes he has nothing for which to vote. No, no we are not satisfied and we will not be satisfied until justice rolls down like waters and righteousness like a mighty stream.

I am not unmindful that some of you have come here out of great trials and tribulations. Some of you have come fresh from narrow jail cells. Some of you have come from areas where your quest for freedom left you battered by storms of persecution and staggered by the winds of police brutality. You have been the veterans of creative suffering. Continue to work with the faith that unearned suffering is redemptive.

Go back to Mississippi, go back to Alabama, go back to South Carolina, go back to Georgia, go back to Louisiana, go back to the slums and ghettos of our northern cities, knowing that somehow this situation can and will be changed.

Let us not wallow in the valley of despair. I say to you today my friends - so even though we face the difficulties of today and tomorrow, I still have a dream. It is a dream deeply rooted in the American dream.

I have a dream that one day this nation will rise up and live out the true meaning of its creed: "We hold these truths to be self-evident, that all men are created equal."

I have a dream that one day on the red hills of Georgia the sons of former slaves and the sons of former slave owners will be able to sit down together at the table of brotherhood.

I have a dream that one day even the state of Mississippi, a state sweltering with the heat of injustice, sweltering with the heat of oppression, will be transformed into an oasis of freedom and justice.

I have a dream that my four little children will one day live in a nation where they will not be judged by the color of their skin but by the content of their character.

I have a dream today.

I have a dream that one day down in Alabama, with its vicious racists, with its governor having his lips dripping with the words of interposition and nullification - one day right there in Alabama little black boys and black girls will be able to join hands with little white boys and white girls as sisters and brothers.

I have a dream today.

I have a dream that one day every valley shall be exalted and every hill and mountain shall be made low, the rough places will be made plain, and the crooked places will be made straight, and the glory of the Lord shall be revealed and all flesh shall see it together.

This is our hope. This is the faith that I go back to the South with. With this faith we will be able to hew out of the mountain of despair a stone of hope. With this faith we will be able to transform the jangling discords of our nation into a beautiful symphony of brotherhood. With this faith we will be able to work together, to pray together, to struggle together, to go to jail together, to stand up for freedom together, knowing that we will be free one day.

This will be the day; this will be the day when all of God's children will be able to sing with new meaning "My country 'tis of thee, sweet land of liberty, of thee I sing. Land where my father's died, land of the Pilgrim's pride, from every mountainside, let freedom ring!"

And if America is to be a great nation, this must become true. And so let freedom ring from the prodigious hilltops of New Hampshire. Let freedom ring from the mighty mountains of New York. Let freedom ring from the heightening Alleghenies of Pennsylvania.

Let freedom ring from the snow-capped Rockies of Colorado. Let freedom ring from the curvaceous slopes of California.

But not only that; let freedom ring from Stone Mountain of Georgia. Let freedom ring from Lookout Mountain of Tennessee. Let freedom ring from every hill and molehill of Mississippi - from every mountainside. Let freedom ring. And when this happens, and when we allow freedom ring - when we let it ring from every village and every hamlet, from every state and every city,

we will be able to speed up that day when all of God's children - black men and white men, Jews and Gentiles, Protestants and Catholics - will be able to join hands and sing in the words of the old Negro spiritual: "Free at last! Free at last! Thank God Almighty, we are free at last!"
-Dr. Martin Luther King

-Leroy Tapia (Texas James)